Cursive Handwriting
Practice with

FAIRY TALES

3 Classic Stories
Letters, Words, and Sentences

Dedicated to my ever-positive daughter,
Piper Gale

How to Use this Workbook:

Trace the letters, words, and sentences first, and then practice writing them in the remaining blank space.

Once they have mastered letters and how to connect letters, feel free to mix and match Parts II and III each day for practice. Combining rote practice with creativity will help maintain their enthusiasm as the story builds.

Each story page in Part III has a corresponding creative drawing page with prompts to inspire and excite your student's imagination. A "Talk about it" question is also included on most doodle drawing pages for reading comprehension, empathy building and emotional regulation, and growing the bond between teacher and student.

Helpful hint: For the reluctant writer, use the doodle pages as a reward at the end of a writing session.

Part I: Letter formation
Part II: Word building from short to long words
Part III: Story sentences, doodle pages, "talk about it" questions

Part One - Letter Formation

Aa Bb Cc Dd Ee

Ff Gg Hh Ii Jj

Kk Ll Mm Nn

Oo Pp Qq Rr Ss

Tt Uu Vv Ww

Xx Yy Zz

Aa Bb Cc Dd Ee Ff Gg Hh Ii Jj Kk Ll Mm Nn Oo Pp Qq Rr Ss Tt Uu Vv Ww Xx Yy Zz

Aa Bb Cc Dd Ee Ff Gg

Hh Ii Jj Kk Ll Mm Nn

Oo Pp Qq Rr Ss Tt Uu

Vv Ww Xx Yy Zz

My Name:

Aa Bb Cc Dd Ee Ff Gg Hh Ii Jj Kk Ll Mm Nn Oo Pp Qq Rr Ss Tt Uu Vv Ww Xx Yy Zz

Aa Bb Cc Dd Ee Ff Gg
Hh Ii Jj Kk Ll Mm Nn
Oo Pp Qq Rr Ss Tt Uu
Vv Ww Xx Yy Zz

My Name:

Part Two - Word Building

Ch ch Ch ch

Sh sh Sh sh

Th th Th th

To to To to

In in In in

Of of Of of

It it It it

Is is Is is

Be be Be be

As as As as

So so So so

We we We we

He he He he

By by By by

On on On on

Do do Do do

Me me Me me

Up up Up up

Go go Go go

No no No no

Aa Bb Cc Dd Ee Ff Gg Hh Ii Jj Kk Ll Mm Nn Oo Pp Qq Rr Ss Tt Uu Vv Ww Xx Yy Zz

Are are

And and

For for

Not not

But but

Had had

Was was

All all

One one

Man man

Aa Bb Cc Dd Ee Ff Gg Hh Ii Jj Kk Ll Mm Nn Oo Pp Qq Rr Ss Tt Uu Vv Ww Xx Yy Zz

Pea pea

Any any

Out out

His his

Her her

Can can

Love love

True true

Once once

Mice mice

Aa Bb Cc Dd Ee Ff Gg Hh Ii Jj Kk Ll Mm Nn Oo Pp Qq Rr Ss Tt Uu Vv Ww Xx Yy Zz

Kind kind

Bold bold

Girl girl

Ball ball

Have have

They they

Come come

Your your

Will will

From from

Aa Bb Cc Dd Ee Ff Gg Hh Ii Jj Kk Ll Mm Nn Oo Pp Qq Rr Ss Tt Uu Vv Ww Xx Yy Zz

Heart heart Heart heart

Fairy fairy Fairy fairy

Smile smile Smile

Dance dance Dance

Laugh laugh Laugh

Aa Bb Cc Dd Ee Ff Gg Hh Ii Jj Kk Ll Mm Nn Oo Pp Qq Rr Ss Tt Uu Vv Ww Xx Yy Zz

Queen queen Queen

Prince prince Prince

Happy happy Happy

Clock clock Clock clock

Moral moral Moral

Carriage carriage

Grateful grateful

Suddenly suddenly

Forever forever

Nibbled nibbled

Aa Bb Cc Dd Ee Ff Gg Hh Ii Jj Kk Ll Mm Nn Oo Pp Qq Rr Ss Tt Uu Vv Ww Xx Yy Zz

Persevere persevere

Delighted delighted

Ridiculous ridiculous

Attention attention

Stepmother stepmother

Aa Bb Cc Dd Ee Ff Gg Hh Ii Jj Kk Ll Mm Nn Oo Pp Qq Rr Ss Tt Uu Vv Ww Xx Yy Zz

Princess princess

Beautiful beautiful

Flowerpot flowerpot

Appearance appearance

Disappoint disappoint

Part Three - Story Sentences

Princess & the Pea

Adapted from Hans Christian Anderson's original story, "Princess and the Pea"

Once upon a time, a prince wanted to marry a true princess. He looked all over, but he could not find one.

A true princess couldn't be found!
Write or draw what you think he
DID find on his adventure:

Talk about it: What would you like to see on
an adventure of your own?

Every time there was
some tiny flaw in a
princess, he would come
home disappointed and
ready to quit looking.

**Write or draw what you think the prince
did to cheer himself up:**

*Talk about it: What do you do to cheer yourself up when you
are feeling disappointed?*

A fierce storm raged one
night. In the middle of
the downpour, there was
a tap-tap-tap knocking
at the palace gate.

Draw a fierce storm:

Talk about it: Have you been caught in a storm before? How did you feel?

Outside stood a
rain-soaked princess
looking awful and
drowned. Yet she said
she was a true princess.

Draw what you think the princess looked like:

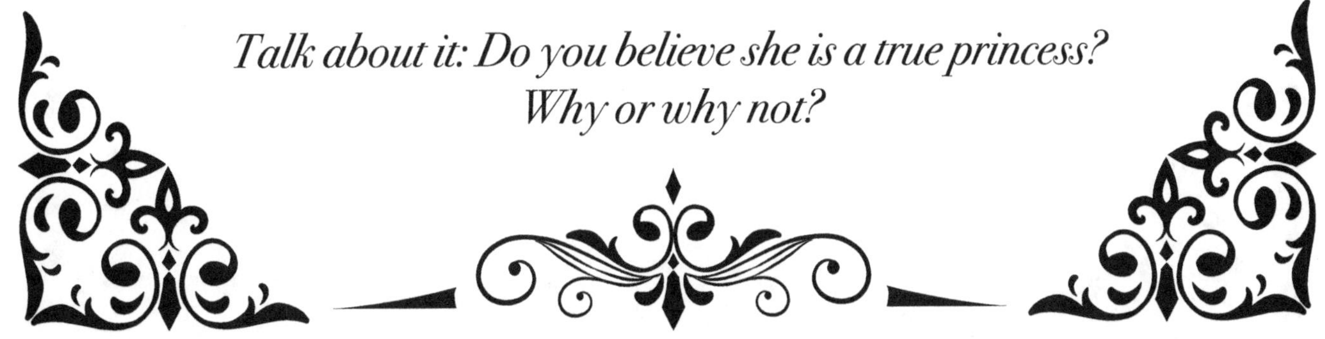

Talk about it: Do you believe she is a true princess?
Why or why not?

The prince's mother was suspicious of her and devised a test. She went quietly into the bedroom provided for the princess.

Draw what you think the prince's mother looked like:

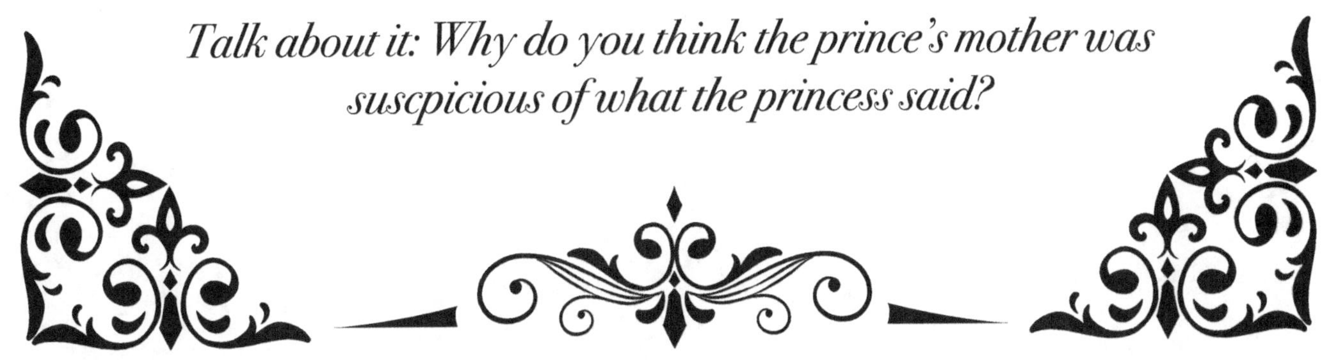

Talk about it: Why do you think the prince's mother was suscpicious of what the princess said?

She laid a tiny pea on
the bottom of the bed.
Then she put twenty
mattresses and fluffy
quilts on top of the pea.

Draw the pea under 20 mattresses and quilts:

Talk about it: Would you like sleeping on top of twenty mattresses and quilts? Why or why not?

It was a fitful night of tossing and turning for the princess. In the morning, she was asked how she had slept.

Write about or draw a time when you couldn't sleep well:

Talk about it: Was there anything you could have done that night to have made it easier to sleep?

"Very badly!" Said the princess. "I laid on something so hard that my whole body was aching. It was terrible!"

**Write or draw how you think the princess
felt after sleeping on the pea:**

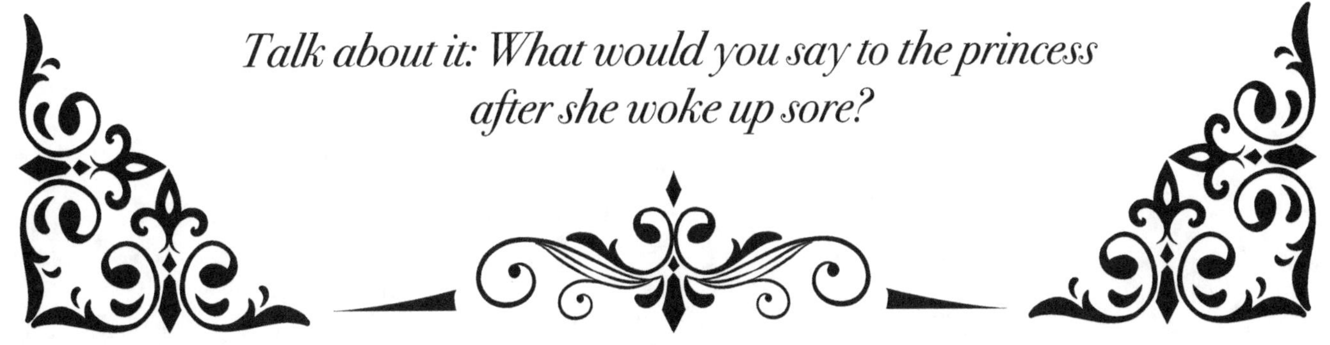

*Talk about it: What would you say to the princess
after she woke up sore?*

She had felt the tiny
pea through the twenty
mattresses and quilts.
Only a true princess
could be so sensitive.

**Write or draw something that bothers
you or makes you upset:**

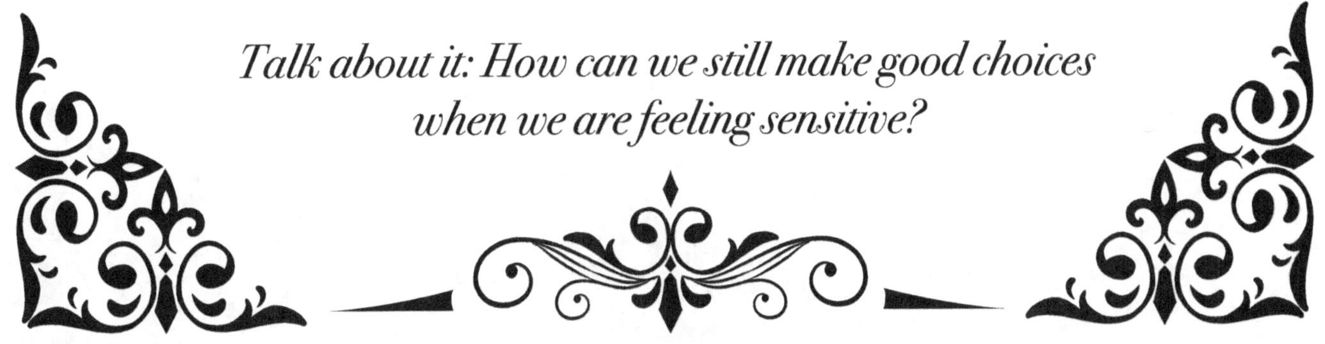

*Talk about it: How can we still make good choices
when we are feeling sensitive?*

So the prince married her, for now he knew she was a true princess despite how she looked that rainy night.

Draw the wedding:

Talk about it: Have you ever changed your mind about someone after you got to know them?

Morals of the story:
Appearances can be
deceiving and little
things can make a big
difference.

Draw your favorite part of the story:

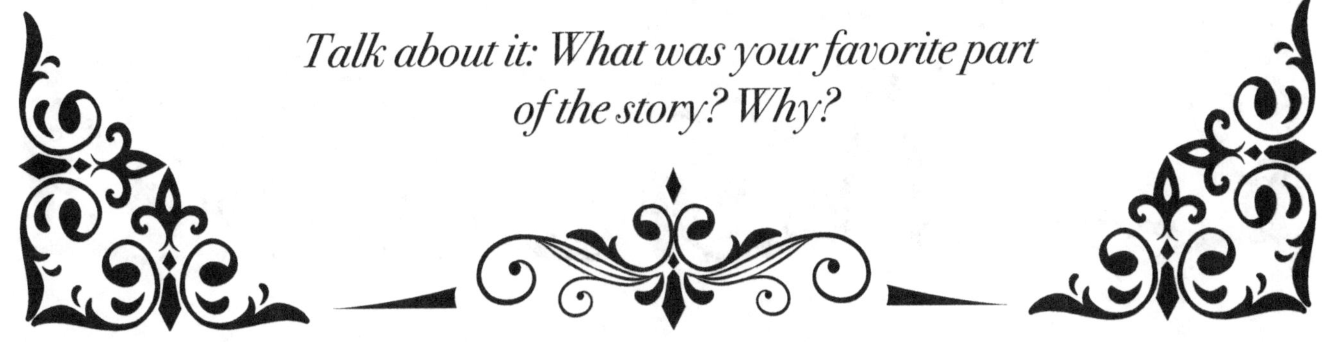

Talk about it: What was your favorite part
of the story? Why?

Thumbelina

Once upon a time, a woman wanted to raise a tiny, little child and asked an old witch where she could obtain one.

Draw something you would really like to have:

Talk about it: Why did you choose what you chose to draw?

"I have one in this seed!
Just put it deep in a
flowerpot, shower with
love, and wait."
Instructed the witch.

Draw what you think the witch looked like:

Talk about it: Would you have trusted the witch?

"Thank you!" Said the woman after paying the witch. Upon planting, a beautiful, budding flower sprouted out of the dirt.

Draw the budding flower in the flowerpot:

In the middle of the bud
sat a tiny, pretty girl.
She was barely half a
thumb tall so they called
her Thumbelina.

Draw what you think Thumbelina looks like:

Talk about it: Why did you choose to draw her the way you did?

One night, an ugly toad crept in and, seeing the girl, exclaimed, "You will make such a pretty bride for my son!"

Draw the most hideous toad you can imagine:

Talk about it: What would you have done if a toad tried to kidnap you?!

She took Thumbelina to a lily pad and hopped off to find her son. The girl woke up surrounded by water and in a fright!

Draw Thumbelina trapped on a lily pad:

Talk about it: How would you feel if you woke up in a strange place?

Thumbelina wept and caught the attention of little fish below. They felt sorry for her and nibbled the lily roots through.

Write about or draw a time when you felt so sad you cried:

Talk about it: What made you feel better?

Away floated the leaf
down the stream, taking
her far from the toads.
She made a home near a
cornfield out of tree bark.

Draw Thumbelina's home near the cornfield:

(Hint: Think about what you could find in the woods or fields to make a teeny, tiny home)

Talk about it: What you are grateful for in your home?

Summer and fall she gathered honey for food and drank the dew off the leaves. Winter came and she was soon freezing.

Write a list or draw the foods you like to eat in the Summer:

Starving, she knocked at
the door of a field mouse.
The mouse had a little
home, warm and snug,
under a corn stalk.

Draw what you think the field mouse looked like:

Talk about it: Do you enjoy sleeping over with friends or family?

The mouse let her stay but said, "You'll have to marry my wealthy friend, Mole. I can not keep providing for you."

How does your family provide for you?
Write a list or draw your home, belongings, and lots of love!

Thumbelina ventured underground to meet Mole. He wasn't kind and he never wanted to feel the warm sun.

**Write a list or draw all the activities you like
to do in the sunshine:**

*Talk about it: Could you live underground for the rest of your life?
Why or why not?*

In one of the tunnels,
she found a sick bird
freezing to death.
After nursing it back to
health it flew off.

**Write about or draw how your loved ones
take care of you when you are feeling ill:**

*Talk about it: What does taking care of the sick bird say
about Thumbelina's character?*

On her wedding day to
Mole, Thumbelina was
filled with dread. All of a
sudden, she heard a
familiar tweet-tweet!

**Write about or draw a time when you
REALLY didn't want to do something:**

Talk about it: How did you get through it?

The once sick bird
appeared and swooped
down to rescue her! She
flew on the bird's back
away to warmer lands.

**Draw Thumbelina soaring through the air
on the back of the bird:**

Talk about it: How do you think it felt to fly through sky?

She chose gorgeous blue
flowers to home in but
was surprised to find a
tiny, handsome man
already living there.

Draw the kind of flowers you would like to live in:

Talk about it: What do you think Thumbelina said when she discovered the flower she chose was already occupied?

Wearing a golden crown and sparkling wings, he greeted her as the King of the Flowers. He was charmed by her.

Draw what you think the King of the Flowers looks like:

*Talk about it: How is the King of the Flowers different
than the toad and mole?*

He spoke gently and
kindly to her, showing
her his flower kingdom.
The people adored him
and she soon did too.

Draw a picture of the kindest person you know:

Talk about it: What makes that person kind?

He placed his own
golden crown on her head
and asked her for her
hand. She responded with
a delighted "Yes!"

Draw a sparkly crown for Thumbelina to wear:

He gifted her a pair of wings so she, too, could fly and called her, "May Blossom, Queen of the Flowers."

Draw fairy wings that you would like to wear:

Talk about it: Why do you think he give her a new name?

Thumbelina lived a
happy life with the King,
grateful to have put the
slimy toad and unkind
mole in her past forever.

Write about or draw a time when you were thankful:

Morals of the story:
You can overcome any obstacle. Stay kind, persevere, and don't be a greedy toad or mole!

Draw your favorite part of the story:

Talk about it: What was your favorite part of the story? Why?

Cinderella

Adapted from Hans Christian Anderson's original story, "Cinderella"

Once upon a time, a sweet, gentle girl named Cinderella lived a hard life. Her widowed father married a wicked lady.

Write about or draw the kind of hard life you think Cinderella lives:

(Hint: What does she do all day? Where does she live? What does she wear?)

Talk about it: What parts of your life are hard?

Her stepsisters were rude and treated her worse than the pigs. When her father suddenly died, their cruelty worsened.

Write about or draw how you feel when someone is mean to you:

Talk about it: How can we still show kindness even when others are mean?

All day, every day, Cinderella cooked, swept, cleaned, washed, fetched, and waited on the women without thanks.

Write a list or draw the kind of chores you do:

*Talk about it: When was the last time you
thanked someone for cleaning? Do it now!*

Her only friends were
the little mice who loved
her singing. She would
also sneak them left-over
crumbs after meals.

Draw Cinderella's mice friends:

Talk about it: Who is your best friend?
What makes them a good friend?

One day, all the ladies in the kingdom were invited to a royal ball where a prince would choose his future wife.

Draw the invitation to the Royal Ball:

Talk about it: How do you think everyone felt
when they opened their invitation?

Cinderella helped the step-sisters try on every dress in the kingdom while wearing tattered, cinder-covered rags.

Draw a ballgown dress that you would want to wear to the royal ball:

Talk about it: Do you think Cinderella was jealous of her stepsisters?

She begged her wicked
stepmother to let her also
attend the royal ball. She
was denied with a
mocking laugh and sneer.

**Write about or draw a place
you really want to visit:**

*Talk about it: What is special about the place
you drew?*

The stepsisters, wearing ridiculous dresses, went to the royal ball while Cinderella was left with a list of chores to do.

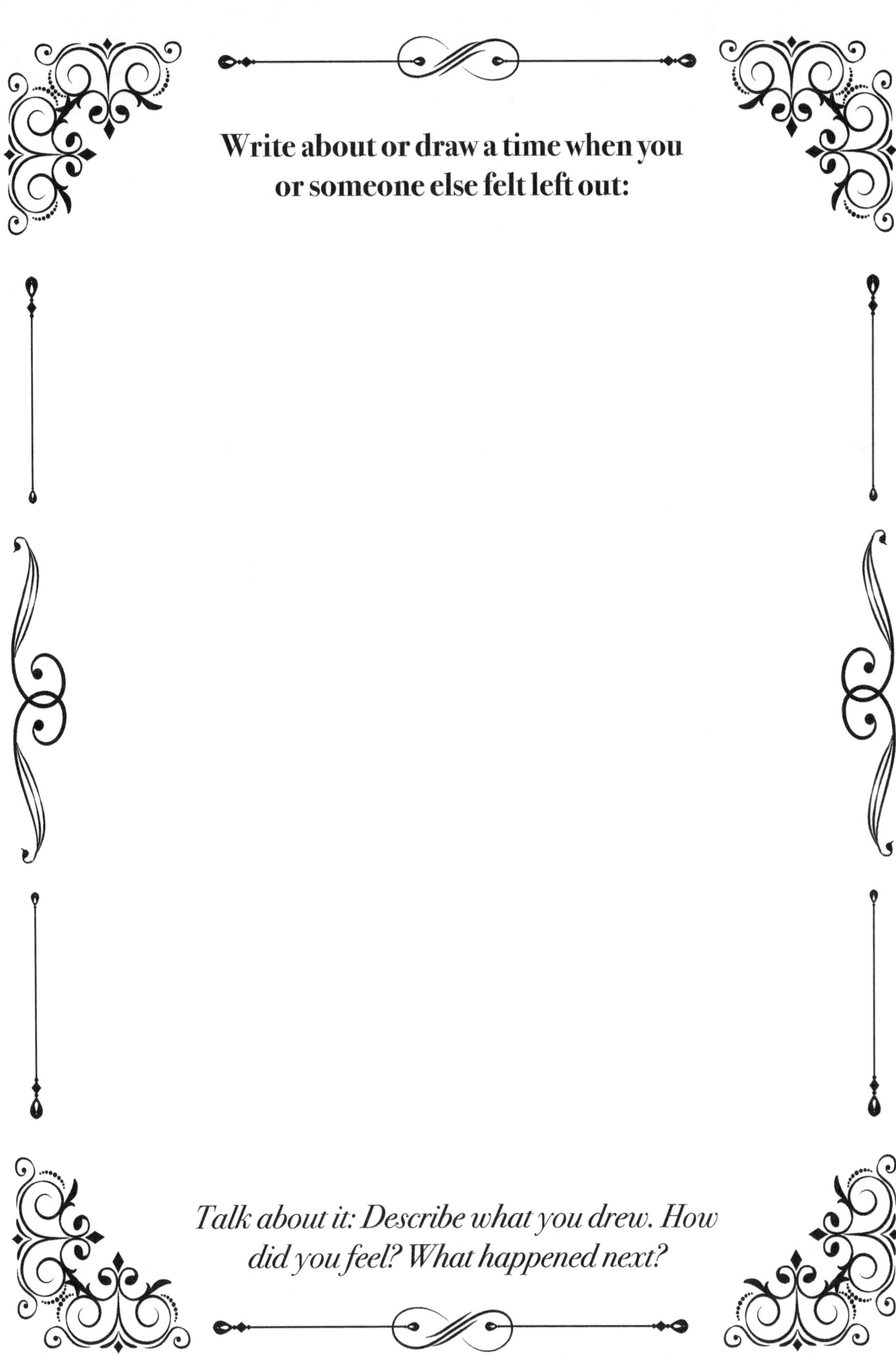

Write about or draw a time when you or someone else felt left out:

Talk about it: Describe what you drew. How did you feel? What happened next?

Suddenly, one of her mouse friends was making a loud racket outside. She went to see what commotion was.

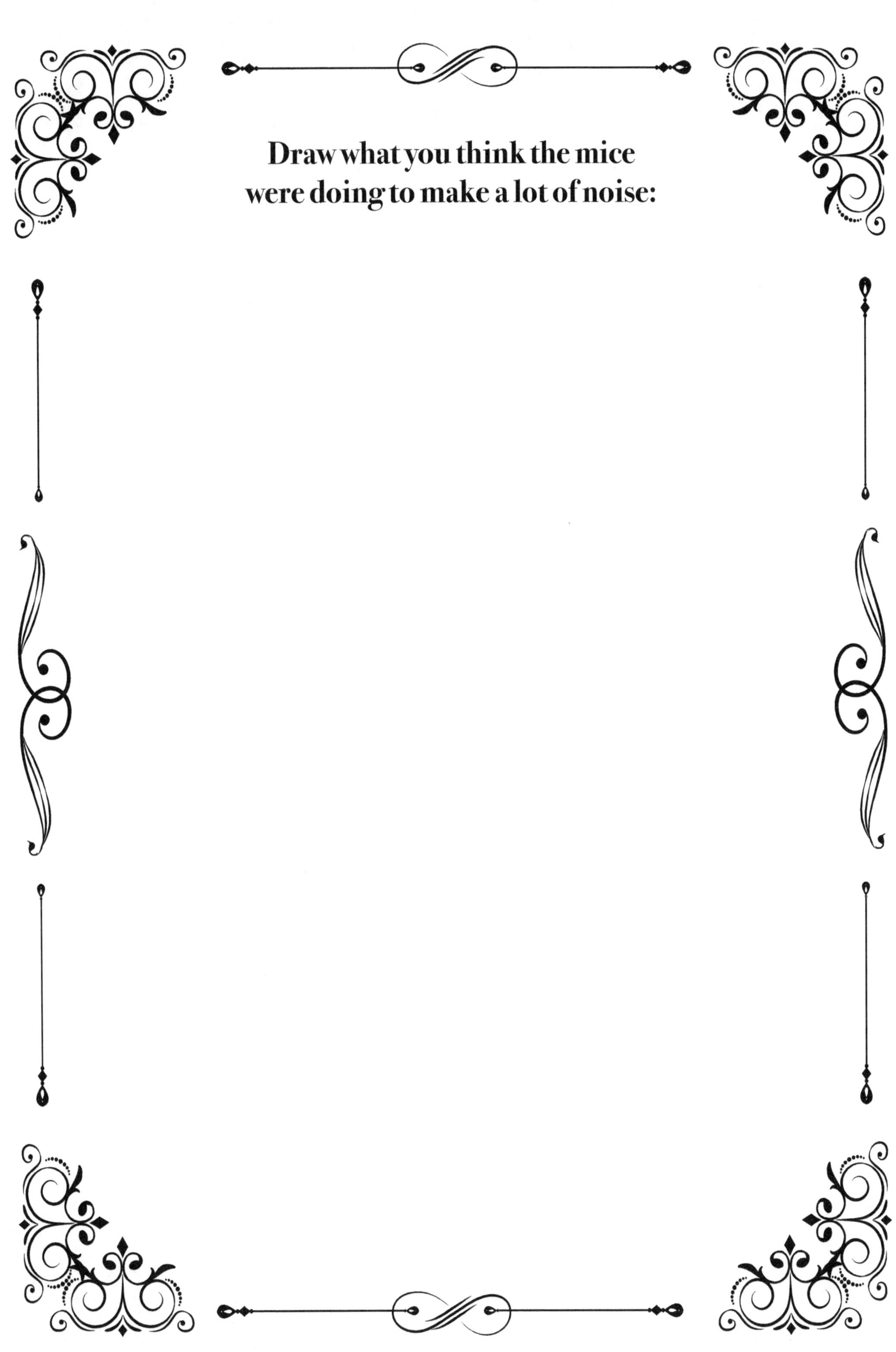

**Draw what you think the mice
were doing to make a lot of noise:**

A beautiful fairy stood in
the garden and told
Cinderella that she was
going to the royal ball to
dance all night!

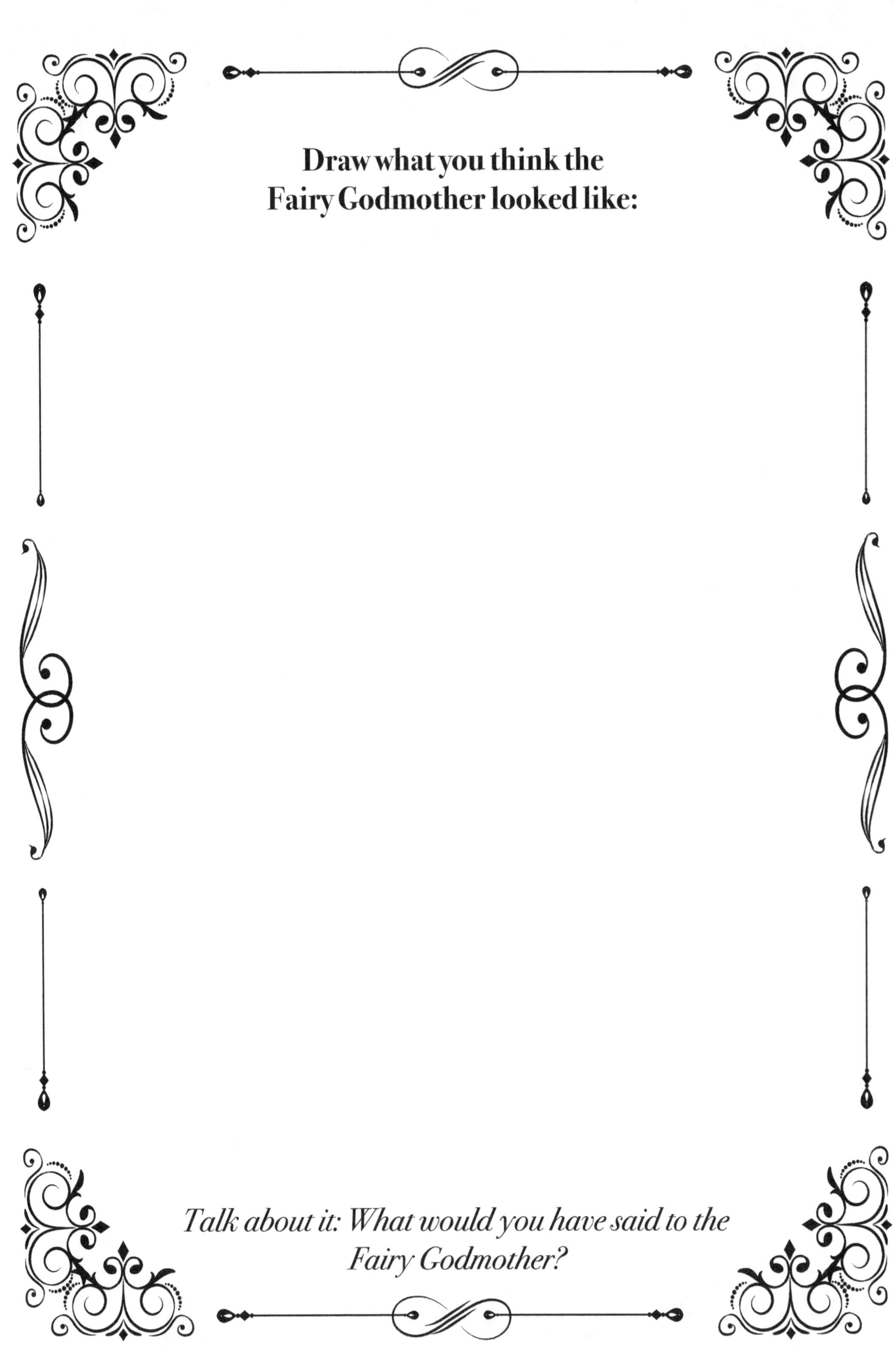

**Draw what you think the
Fairy Godmother looked like:**

*Talk about it: What would you have said to the
Fairy Godmother?*

A pumpkin turned into a carriage, mice into footmen, and Cinderella's rags into a beautiful gown and glass slippers.

Draw the carriage and Cinderella's beautiful dress:

*Talk about it: How do you think Cinderella felt
when everything transformed around her?*

"Leave before the clock strikes midnight!" The Fairy Godmother instructed and, with that, the carriage took off.

Draw a clock striking midnight:

Talk about it: What happens when we don't
listen to instructions?

All eyes were on her as she entered the Royal Ballroom, including the Prince's. He asked her to dance again and again.

Draw what you think the ballroom looked like:

(Hint: Think about decorations, food, people, costumes, etc)

Talk about it: How do you think Cinderella felt when she walked into the ballroom?

Between dances, chats, and laughs they fell in love. He was about to ask her to marry him when the clock struck!

Write about or draw what you and your best friend like to do when you are together:

Talk about it: How do you feel when you get to visit that good friend?

Cinderella ran from the castle so quickly that she left one of her glass slippers. Later, the Prince found it on the stairs.

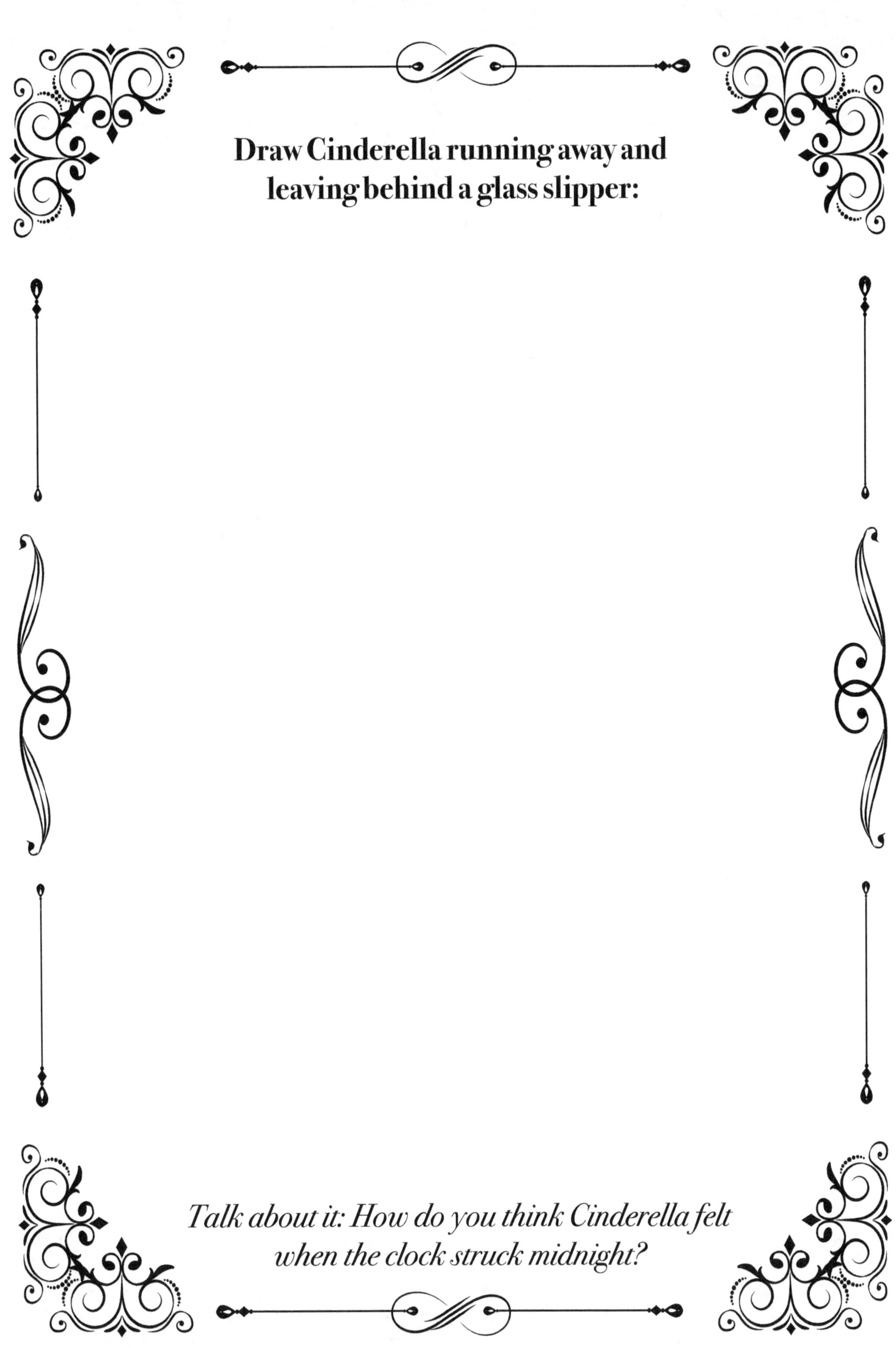

**Draw Cinderella running away and
leaving behind a glass slipper:**

*Talk about it: How do you think Cinderella felt
when the clock struck midnight?*

Heartsick, the Prince ordered every lady in the kingdom to try the glass slipper until they found the perfect match.

Draw a broken heart:

Talk about it: Have you ever missed someone so much it hurt?

Cinderella's rude stepsisters pushed and shoved to try on the slipper, but it did not fit either of their feet.

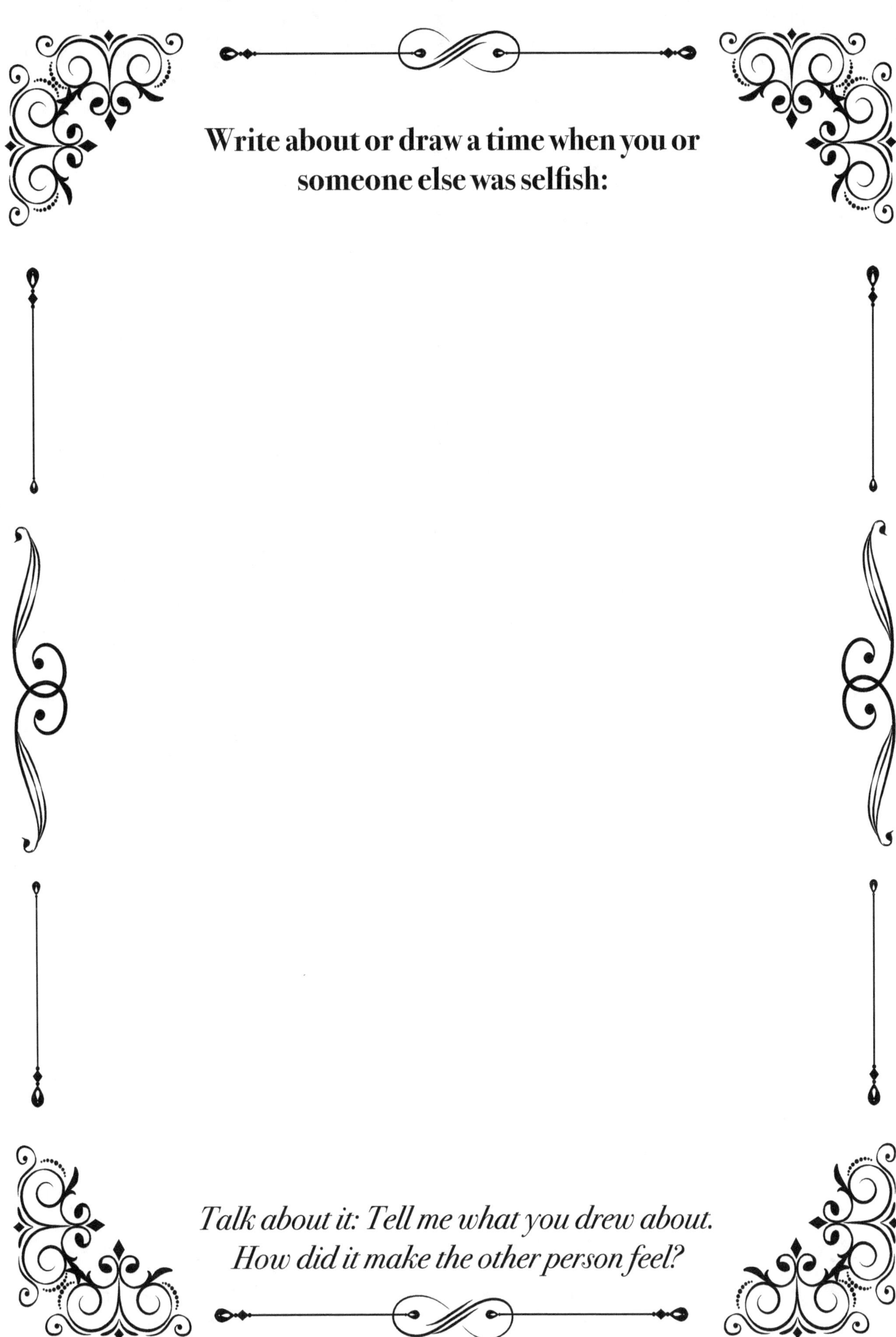

Write about or draw a time when you or someone else was selfish:

Talk about it: Tell me what you drew about.
How did it make the other person feel?

A royal servant noticed a girl covered in cinders sweeping and asked her to try on the slipper. The stepmother scoffed.

Draw Cinderella sweeping the floor:

*Talk about it: Why doesn't the stepmother think
Cinderella should try on the slipper?*

Her foot glided in for a perfect fit. The stepmother and sisters' jaws dropped and they began to yell unkind things.

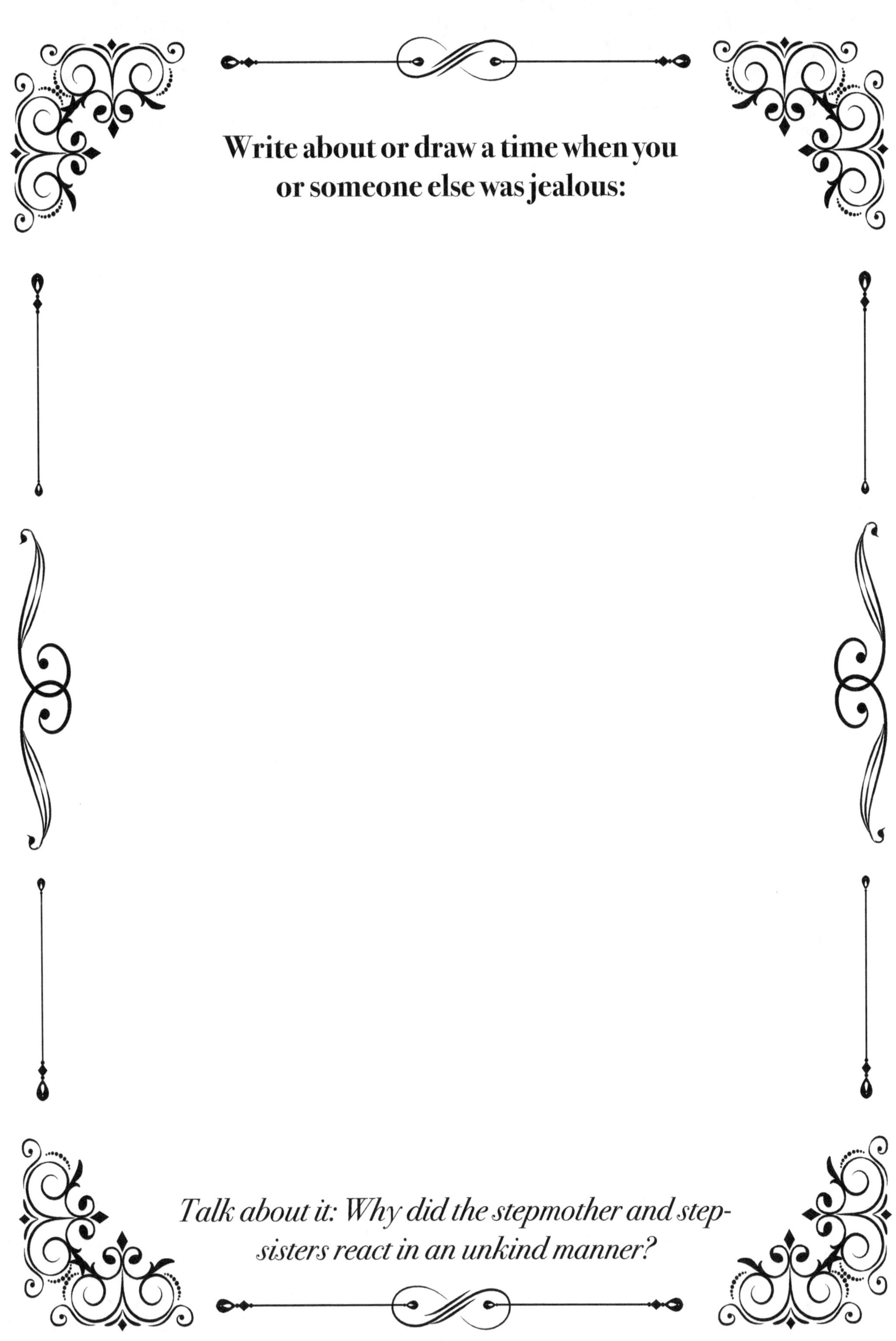

Write about or draw a time when you or someone else was jealous:

Talk about it: Why did the stepmother and step-sisters react in an unkind manner?

But the royal servant
and Cinderella heard
none of it as they rode
off in a carriage to the
castle, rags and all.

Draw the castle:

Talk about it: How do you think Cinderella felt as they rode away from her home and to the castle?

Before seeing the glass slipper, the Prince knew it was Cinderella, his love, despite the cinders covering her torn dress.

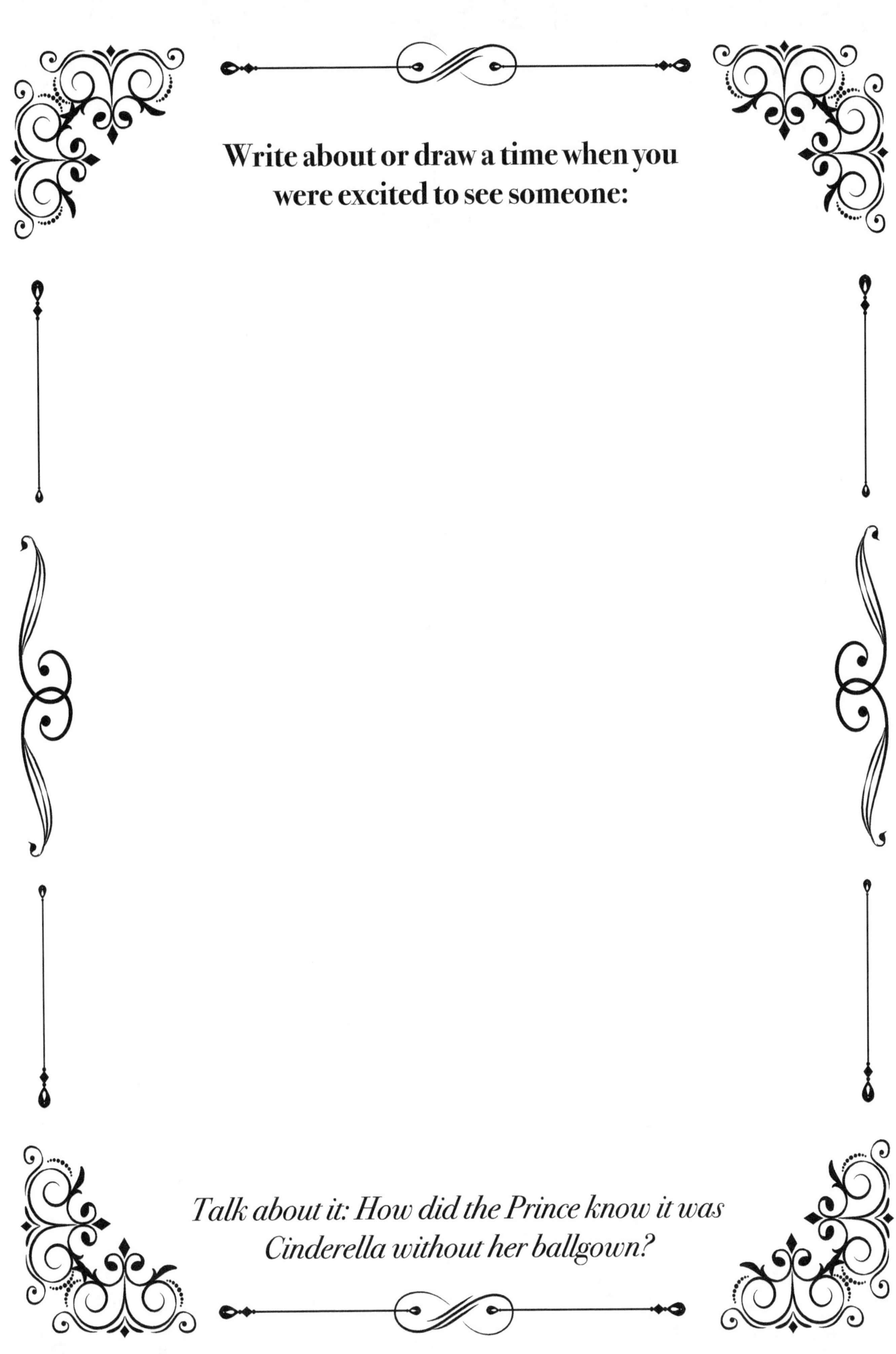

**Write about or draw a time when you
were excited to see someone:**

*Talk about it: How did the Prince know it was
Cinderella without her ballgown?*

Cinderella and the Prince's love grew and they wed soon after. She, of course, wore the glass slippers down the aisle.

Draw Cinderella's wedding:

Morals of the story:
Never stop dreaming, be
brave, and take chances.
Always be kind no
matter a person's status.

Draw your favorite part of the story:

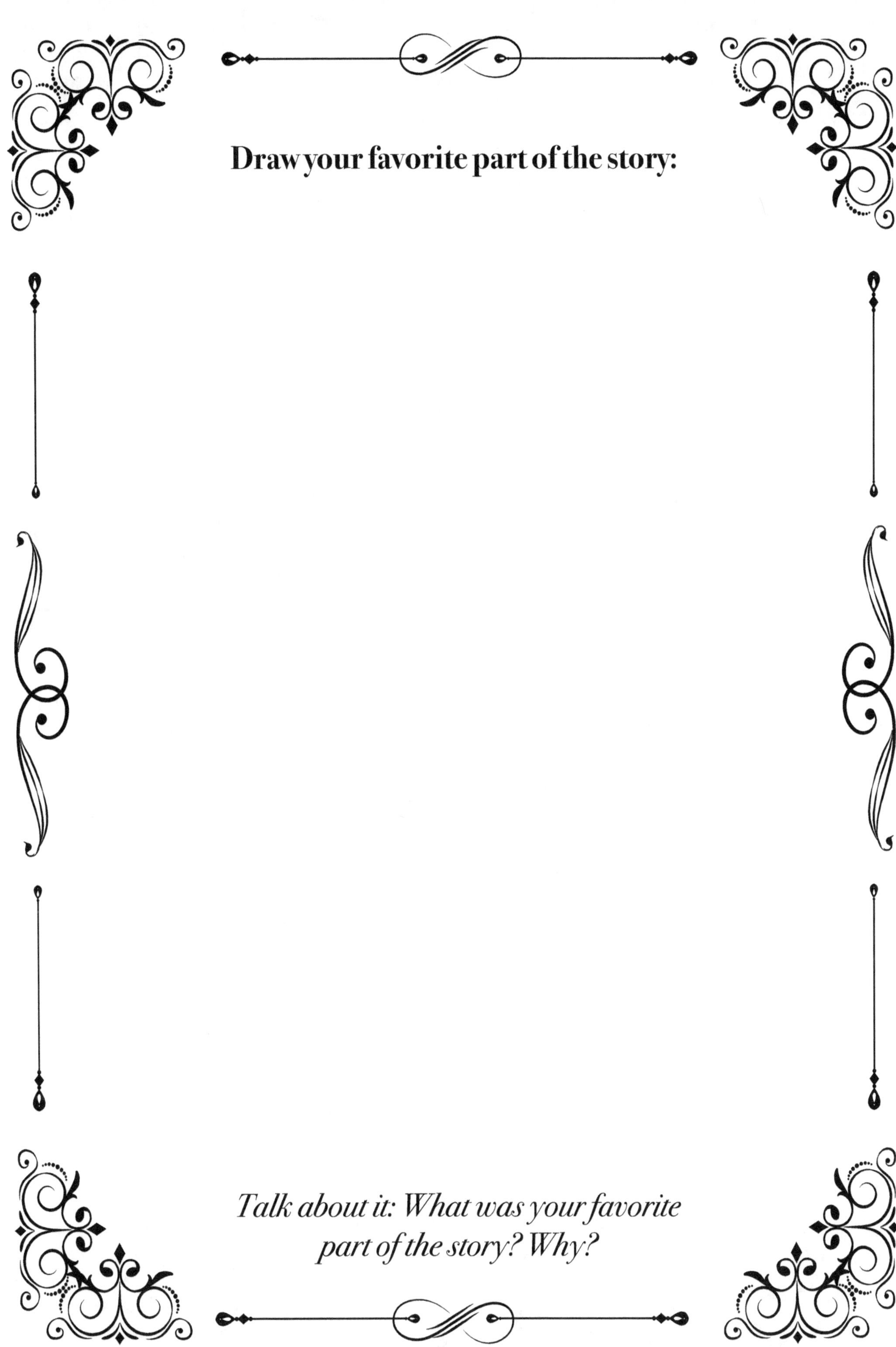

Talk about it: What was your favorite part of the story? Why?

Fun fact: The Piper Maria LLC logo was created from my six year old daughter's cursive handwriting. She was the inspiration for this book and continually reminds me to mix in a little positivity and creativity when doing hard things.